Why Is This Day Special?

A Wedding

Jillian Powell

W

FRANKLIN WATTS

LONDON·SYDNEY

First published in 2005 by Franklin Watts
96 Leonard Street, London EC2A 4XD

Franklin Watts Australia
45-51 Huntley Street
Alexandria, NSW 2015

© Franklin Watts 2005

Series editor: Sarah Peutrill
Art director: Jonathan Hair
Designer: Ian Thompson
Picture researcher: Diana Morris
Reading consultant: Margaret Perkins, Institute of
Education, University of Reading

A CIP catalogue record for this book is available from the
British Library

ISBN 0 7496 6023 6

Printed in Dubai

Picture credits: Mark Antman/Image Works/Topham: 11t.
Annie Griffiths-Belt/Corbis: 25t. Jonathan Blair/Corbis: 23.
Stephen Cannerelli/Image Works/Topham: 27c. DPA/Image
Works/Topham: 13t, 14, 18. Hulton Deutsch/Corbis: 19b.
Hurewitz Creative/Corbis: 3. Chris Fairclough/Franklin
Watts: 8b. Image Works/Topham: 4. Michael Justice/Image
Works/Topham: 12. Kent Meiris/Image Works/Topham: 9b,
17t. Ray Moller/Franklin Watts: Front cover bottom, 15tr,
20b, 21tl, 21b, 22, 26t, 27t. Novosti/Topham: 24.
Picturepoint/Topham: 5t. Spinning your dreams: Front cover
main, 7b, 10, 15t, 19m, 25b, 26b. Zev Radovan, Israel: 13b.
Zefa: 17b. Teake Zuidema/Image Works/Topham: 15b.
Every attempt has been made to clear copyright. Should
there be any inadvertent omission please apply to the
publisher for rectification.

With many thanks to the following for permission to use
photographs: Spinning Your Dreams wedding photograpy
(www.spinningyourdreams.co.uk), Russell Holdsworth,
Nicola Kolndreu, Lisa Gooch, Raj and Suzannah Trivedi and
Irene Peutrill for the painting on page 8.

Contents

Two people

A wedding day is often the happiest day in someone's life. It is a day they will always remember.

It is an important day because it is the start of a new life for two people. It joins their lives together in law, and sometimes in religion.

> *" When I grow up, I want a really big wedding with all my family and hundreds of guests! I often dream about it. "*
>
> *Shobna, aged 9*

When they are married, the couple will live together and share everything they own. They may have children together.

A couple sign a register at their Christian wedding. This means that they are now married in law.

Some people have a quiet wedding, with just a few relatives or friends.

A couple in Borneo have a small simple wedding with their family.

Other couples choose a big wedding with lots of guests.

The couple at this wedding chose to celebrate with a big group of friends and family.

Getting ready

Before a couple get married there are a lot of things they need to do.

When the couple set a date for their wedding, they send out invitations to their family and friends.

Invitation to the wedding of Louise Burns and Peter Thomas at All Saints' Church.

If a couple choose to have a Christian wedding, banns may be called in church. This means that on three Sundays, the vicar announces their wedding and asks if anyone knows of a reason why the couple may not marry.

A Christian curate signs a certificate to say the banns have been read in church. This means the wedding can go ahead.

The couple choose the people who will play a special part in the ceremony. There may be a best man and bridesmaids or pages.

The couple will also choose their clothes and decorations, and food for the wedding feast or reception.

" I was really excited when my sister asked me to be her bridesmaid. We chose my dress together. It was in red satin. "

Lauren, aged 12

A Japanese bride gets ready for her wedding.

On the big day the bride and groom may get ready apart and only see each other at the ceremony.

Ceremonies

Weddings can have a religious or a civil ceremony.

A bride and groom follow a Christian ceremony in a church.

Many people who belong to a religion get married in a holy place such as a church, mosque or synagogue.

In some countries they can also have a religious ceremony in a park or garden.

> " *My sister was married in our mosque. It's a really special place for our family because we visit it every week.* "
>
> Mina, aged 8

Jewish ceremonies are held in a synagogue, park or garden. The bride and groom may stand under a huppah for the ceremony.

The huppah stands for the home the couple will make together.

A couple are married in a civil ceremony on a beach in Mauritius.

Some people have a civil ceremony. They may get married in a public building called a registry office.

Others have a civil ceremony in a beautiful setting such as a grand house or garden, or on a beach. People can even get married at a sports ground, in a castle or on a submarine!

Vows

The most important part of a wedding ceremony is when the couple say their vows. These are promises to each other.

The couple promise to love and look after each other, and to stay together for the rest of their lives.

They say their vows in front of the person who is marrying them, and their friends and family.

" My brother was so worried that he would make a mistake when he said his vows. He practised a lot! "

Kofi, aged 8

A Muslim couple make their vows at their wedding ceremony in Malaysia.

In a Hindu wedding, the bride and groom say their vows as they take seven steps around a sacred fire. They say one vow with each step they take.

A Hindu couple in front of a sacred fire.

The marriage contract is read at a Jewish wedding in Jerusalem.

In Jewish and Muslim weddings, the couple sign a marriage contract. This sets out the rules that they will follow when they are married.

13

Tying the knot

Marriage is sometimes called 'tying the knot' as two people are joined together in law and religion.

In Hindu weddings, the priest ties the groom's scarf to the bride's sari to show they are joined together for life.

> *I went to a Hindu wedding last year. It's called Ganthibandhan when the priest ties the wedding knot.*
> Parvesh, aged 9

Then the bride and groom give each other garlands.

A Hindu couple give each other garlands made from flowers. Sometimes the garlands are made from fruit, ribbons or beads.

In many ceremonies the couple give each other wedding rings to show that their love will last forever. In British weddings, the groom puts the wedding ring on the third finger of his bride's left hand.

People once believed that this finger was linked to the heart.

In Orthodox Christian weddings the couple wear crowns, which are joined together by a ribbon.

A Greek Orthodox wedding in the USA. The joining of the crowns stands for the couple's marriage.

What they wear

There are many different traditions for the clothes worn at weddings.

Colour is important. In the West, it is traditional for brides to wear white as the colour of purity. They sometimes wear a veil over the head.

The bride may wear the veil over her face during the ceremony. The groom lifts it over her head when they are married.

This bride is wearing a white dress and veil.

In Asia, brides often wear red as this is the colour of blood or life.

Japanese brides often wear a white kimono for the ceremony. Later they change into a brightly-coloured kimono.

> **"** *My sister had lovely kimonos for her wedding because in Japan the bride changes clothes.* **"**
>
> *Keiko, aged 8*

This bride's kimono is covered with flowers. The groom wears a traditional black kimono.

Some Sikh grooms wear a veil with a golden fringe that covers the face.

A Sikh couple exchange garlands at their wedding.

The bride

There are many old customs which people believe bring a bride good luck.

Before their wedding, Asian brides may have their hands and feet painted with patterns in mehndi, or henna.

" When my sister was married, we had a henna night at our house. My aunt mixed up the henna, and painted everyone's hands. I had my hands painted too. "

Sujata, aged 8

A Muslim bride's hands decorated with mehndi for her marriage.

18

Flowers are carried as a bouquet or worn as garlands or in a headdress.

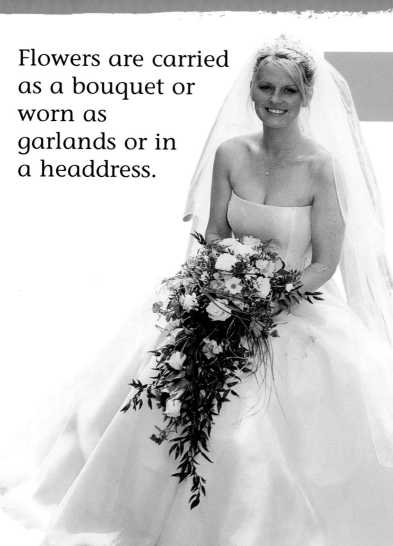

There may be bridesmaids to help the bride. Sometimes the bridesmaid holds the train or carries the bride's bouquet.

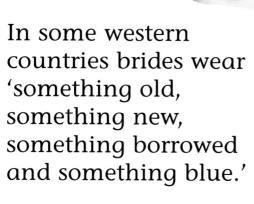

In some western countries brides wear 'something old, something new, something borrowed and something blue.'

In the past some brides invited a chimney sweep to their wedding to bring good luck.

A chimney sweep wishing a bride luck in her married life, 1956.

Good luck

There are many different customs to wish a couple luck and happiness in their married life together.

At Chinese weddings 'double happiness' banners are displayed for good luck.

> **"** *At a wedding I went to, they tied horseshoes to the bride and groom's car to wish them luck when they went on their honeymoon.* **"**
>
> *Amy, aged 9*

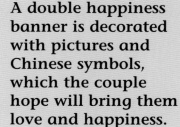

A double happiness banner is decorated with pictures and Chinese symbols, which the couple hope will bring them love and happiness.

Guests often throw rice or confetti over a couple to wish them many children.

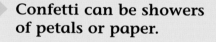

Confetti can be showers of petals or paper.

At Sikh and Hindu weddings, coconuts are given to the couple for luck.

People hope the coconuts will also bring the couple a big family.

In Poland, the parents of the bride and groom give them bread and salt at the reception. The bread is so that they never go hungry. The salt reminds them that they will have hard times.

Bread and salt are given for good luck at a Polish wedding.

Cards and gifts

Family and friends celebrate a wedding by giving cards and gifts to the couple.

After Muslim ceremonies, sweet foods are given to the bride and groom by each other's family, to welcome them into the family.

A Muslim bride and groom are given sweet foods such as dried dates.

Sometimes, a couple write a 'wedding list' of things they would like. Wedding guests can choose what to buy from the list.

The bride and groom may receive presents from their family and friends.

The wedding presents may be set out on a table at the reception for everyone to see.

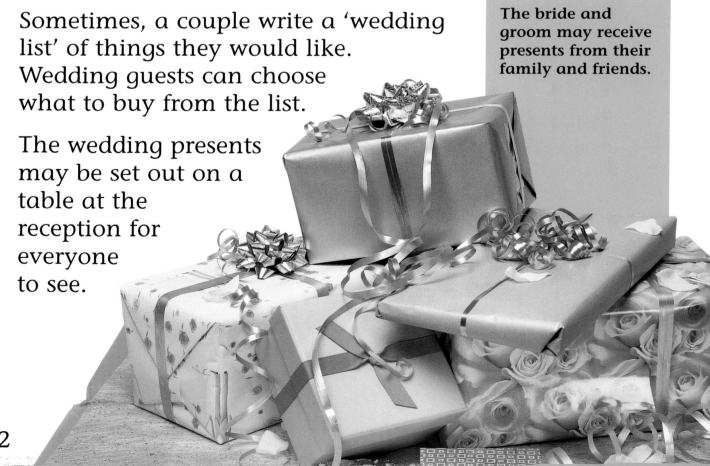

A couple wear gifts of paper money at their wedding in Cyprus.

In Mexico, and some European countries, guests pin money to the bride and groom for a 'money dance' at the reception. This is to bring them luck and good fortune in their married life.

> **66** *At my cousin's Sikh wedding, we all threw flower petals and gave them gifts before they went to the temple for a blessing.* **99**
>
> *Suresh, aged 9*

Parties and receptions

Many people celebrate weddings with a party or reception after the ceremony.

The reception can be held at a hotel or at home. There are decorations, lots of food and drink, and music for dancing. People drink toasts to wish the couple happiness.

> " *If I ever get married I'd like a big party with lots of dancing.* "
> *Leila, aged 12*

At a Russian wedding the party is a very important part of the wedding. It can last for two days!

This Russian groom leads the dancing at his wedding reception.

This Jewish couple hold a handkerchief, which shows they have been joined in marriage.

At a Jewish wedding reception the bride and groom sometimes sit on a chair, holding either end of a handkerchief, and the guests lift them into the air.

After a wedding feast, there is often a wedding cake. The bride and groom cut the first piece of cake together to show that they are starting out on a new life as one.

A couple smile for the camera as they cut the first slice of their wedding cake.

Remembering the day

A couple will always remember their wedding day.

Just afterwards they may send a piece of wedding cake to friends who could not go to the wedding.

There are many ways of keeping memories. Brides may keep their wedding dress or headdress, or have their wedding bouquet dried so it lasts forever.

The bride and groom can choose many types of flowers. They are a very special part of their day, which they will want to remember.

The couple may also make an album of their wedding photographs, or keep a film of the wedding.

A wedding album contains treasured memories.

This couple are celebrating their diamond anniversary, after 60 years together.

Every year, the couple may celebrate their wedding anniversary. Paper gifts are sometimes given for a first anniversary.

After 25 years, the couple celebrate their Silver anniversary.

They may even reach their Golden anniversary marking 50 years together!

" My Nan and Grandad had their golden wedding anniversary last year. We had a big family party. "
Paula, aged 9

27

Glossary

Anniversary marks the date when a wedding took place.

Banns an announcement of a wedding made in church three times, to ask if there is any reason why the couple cannot marry.

Best man a friend of the groom who takes care of the wedding ring.

Bouquet a beautiful arrangement of flowers.

Ceremony the formal part of a wedding when a couple's vows are made.

Civil ceremony a wedding that is not religious.

Confetti showers of paper or flower petals thrown at a wedding.

Curate an assistant to a vicar in a Christian church.

Custom an act that is repeated over many years.

Huppah a Jewish wedding canopy.

Mehndi a red dye made from henna.

Reception a feast or party held after a wedding ceremony.

Registry office a building where civil weddings take place.

Sacred something that is holy or blessed.

Sari traditional dress for Asian women.

Toast a wish for happiness or congratulations, made by raising a glass of drink.

Veil a piece of material that covers the head.

Vows solemn promises.

Religions in this book

Christianity
Follower: Christian
Important figure: Jesus Christ, Son of God
God: One God as Father, Son and Holy Spirit
Places of worship: Churches, cathedrals and chapels
Holy book: The Bible

Hinduism
Follower: Hindu
Gods: Many gods and goddesses, including Brahma, the Creator, Vishnu, the Protector and Shiva, the Destroyer
Places of worship: Mandirs (temples) and shrines
Holy books: Vedas, Upanishads, Ramayana, Mahabharata

Islam
Follower: Muslim
Important figure: The Prophet Muhammad
God: Allah
Place of worship: Mosque
Holy book: The Qur'an

Judaism
Follower: Jew
Important figures: Abraham, Isaac, Jacob and Moses
God: One God, the creator
Place of Worship: Synagogues
Holy Books: Tenakh, Torah, Talmud

Sikhism
Follower: Sikh
Important figure: Guru Nanak
Gods: One God
Place of worship: Gurdwaras (temples)
Holy book: Guru Granth Sahib

Index

Material Matters
Wood

Terry Jennings

Chrysalis Children's Books

First published in the UK in 2003 by
Chrysalis Children's Books
64 Brewery Road
London N7 9NT

© Chrysalis Books Plc 2003

Text by Terry Jennings

ISBN 1-84138-822-X

British Library Cataloguing in Publication Data
for this book is available from the British Library.

A Belitha Book

Editorial Manager: Joyce Bentley
Series Editor: Sarah Nunn
Design: Stonecastle Graphics Ltd
Picture Researcher: Paul Turner

Printed in China

10 9 8 7 6 5 4 3 2 1

Picture credits:
Caffeinebuzz: page 20.
Corbis: page 23 @ Hulton-Deutsch Collection/Corbis.
Roddy Paine Photographic Studios: pages 5, 12, 14, 15 (top), 16-17, 28-29.
Spectrum Colour Library: page 9 (below).
Stonecastle Graphics: pages 15 (below), 25, 26.
Sylvia Cordaiy Photo Library: pages 9 (top), 18, 22.
Terry Jennings: pages 4, 6-7, 10, 11 (below), 19, 24.

Contents

The wood we use

Wood comes from the **trunks** and branches of **trees**. The wood is underneath the bark of the tree.

The walls of this house in Austria are made from wood. All houses contain a lot of wood.

4

The world's tallest tree was over 130 metres high.

Much of our furniture is made from wood.

Lots of musical instruments, like a guitar, are made from wood.

Wood is used to make many things like furniture, boxes, fences and toys. It is also used to make telegraph poles, pencils and paper. Wood can be easily cut, shaped and coloured.

Trees and wood

Broad-leaved trees, like these sycamores, grow very slowly.

Some of our wood comes from trees like oak, ash, beech, teak and maple. These trees have leaves that fall off in winter.

An oak tree may still be growing when it is 100 years old.

But most of the wood we use comes from trees such as pine and spruce, which have their seeds in cones. These trees, called **conifers**, grow quite quickly. They are often planted in special forests called **plantations**.

Every year a tree grows a new layer of wood. If you count all the rings in the trunk of a cut tree, you can tell how many years old it is.

Nowadays, much of our wood comes from trees such as the pines in this plantation.

Felling a tree

The people who cut down trees are called **lumberjacks**. They use special motor saws, called chainsaws, to cut down the trees. In some plantations, big machines cut down all the trees.

A lumberjack knows how and where to cut a tree to make it fall exactly where he wants.

Once a tree has been cut down, it is taken away to a **sawmill**. Most tree trunks are carried to the sawmill on special lorries or trains.

These tree trunks are being floated down a river to the sawmill.

An oak tree may use 200 litres of water in a day. (This would make 800 cups of tea!)

In some countries, elephants or horses are used to pull the tree trunks out of the forest.

9

Making planks

At the sawmill huge saws cut the tree trunks into thin slices, called **planks**.

The heaviest wood is ironwood from South Africa. It sinks if you put it in water.

Planks and tree trunks piled high at a sawmill.

Before the planks can be used, they have to be dried. This is called **seasoning**. If wood is not seasoned, it may later bend, twist or split. Sometimes the wood is seasoned in the open air. Sometimes it is dried quickly in a special oven called a **kiln**.

Tree trunks being sliced into planks.

These planks are being seasoned in the open air. It takes a long time to season wood this way.

11

Beautiful wood

Pieces of wood from different kinds of trees are different colours. They also have different patterns on them.

This box was decorated with pieces of wood that have different patterns on them.

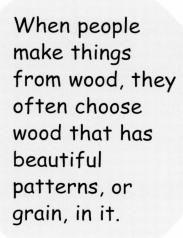

When people make things from wood, they often choose wood that has beautiful patterns, or grain, in it.

Wood is made up of lots of long, thin threads called **fibres**. The pattern the fibres make is called the **grain** of the wood. Sometimes there are **knots** in a piece of wood. They show where a branch joined the trunk of the tree.

Other kinds of wood

Not all logs are cut into planks. Some logs have a beautiful grain that makes them very valuable. These logs may be cut into very thin slices called **veneers**. The veneer is then glued over cheaper pieces of wood.

A lot of furniture is made from veneered wood.

Even small pieces of wood are not wasted. Chipboard is made from tiny scraps of wood glued together in big sheets.

Plywood is made by sticking thin sheets of wood together.

This games board and box have been made using thin veneers of wood.

Working with wood

It is quite easy to cut wood into different shapes to make things. A person who makes things from wood is called a **carpenter**.

A carpenter working in a well-equipped workshop.

16

A carpenter uses special tools to cut and shape wood. He rubs the pieces smooth with sandpaper. Then the pieces are joined together with glue, nails or screws. He may then paint or varnish the wood.

Sharp tools like this chisel are used to shape wood.

Wood as a fuel

In many parts of the world, wood is an important **fuel**. It is burned to give heat for cooking or to keep people warm.

This woman in Africa is collecting wood to make a fire for cooking.

Another important fuel is **charcoal**. Charcoal is made from wood. At barbecues, people cook their food over burning charcoal.

Charcoal is made by partly burning wood in a special oven, or kiln, like this. After several days, the wood will turn into black charcoal.

Wood pulp and paper

A lot of wood from plantations is made into paper. The wood is chopped into tiny pieces called wood chips.

These wood chips are ready to be made into paper.

The wood chips are then mixed with chemicals and heated to make a wet **pulp**. Heavy rollers press the pulp into a thin sheet. Hot rollers dry the paper, which is then wound onto huge reels.

Wasps make their nests from paper. They chew up wood to make a pulp, which then hardens into paper as it dries.

Paper being made in a paper mill.

New materials from wood

Rubber is obtained from the bark of a rubber tree. A cut is made in the bark and the white sticky liquid that comes out is made into rubber.

Some wood pulp is turned into a material called **rayon**, or artificial silk. Until rayon was discovered, all clothes were made from wool, silk or fur, which comes from animals, or they were made from cotton from the cotton plant.

Today, rayon is sometimes used to make clothes and scarves.

This picture shows workers in a rayon factory in 1926.

23

Wood rots

When a tree dies, insects and **fungi** feed on the wood. They make it slowly **rot** away. The remains of the wood go into the soil where they help other plants to grow.

Some fungi are poisonous. The world's most poisonous fungus is called the Death Cap.

Fungi growing on a dead tree.

The wood used in furniture and buildings will also rot. To stop this happening, we paint or varnish the wood. This keeps insects and fungi away. It also makes the wood look bright and shiny.

This wooden arch is being varnished to stop it from rotting.

Wood for the future

Wood is a valuable **material**. We must use it, and paper, carefully. In some countries, people are cutting down trees faster than new ones can grow. We must plant new trees whenever we can.

The trees that give us wood are beautiful. They also give food and shelter to animals and help to clean the air we breathe.

One tree is cut down to make just 400 copies of a newspaper.

New paper can be made from waste paper by **recycling** it. For every tonne of waste paper we recycle, we save 17 trees from being cut down.

Do it yourself

Looking at wood

1 Collect a number of small pieces of wood. An adult may be able to help you.

2 See how hard or soft your pieces of wood are. Try to scratch them with a coin, and then with a metal nail. Which pieces of wood are the hardest to scratch? Which pieces scratch easily?

3 Now put your pieces of wood in a bowl of water. Which pieces float? Which pieces sink? Do some pieces float higher in the water than others?

4 Do all your pieces of wood look the same when they are wet as they do when they are dry?

Glossary

carpenter Someone who makes things out of wood.

charcoal A black or dark grey substance made from partly burned wood.

conifer A type of tree, like a pine or fir, that bears cones.

fibres Long, thin, hair-like strands of material.

fuel Any material that will burn and produce heat.

fungus A living thing, a kind of mushroom or toadstool, that grows on other living things or on rotting material.

grain The pattern of lines on a piece of wood.

kiln A large oven.

knot A round spot on a piece of wood where there was once a branch.

lumberjack A person whose job is to cut down trees.

materials The substances from which things are made.

plank A long, flat piece of cut wood.

plantation An area of land where trees have been planted by people.

pulp A soft, wet mass of wood from which paper is made.

rayon Artificial silk.

recycle To treat waste material so that it can be used again.

rot To go soft or bad so that the object is useless.

sawmill A factory where tree trunks are cut into planks.

seasoning The slow, careful drying of wood before it can be used.

tree A large, woody plant.

trunk The woody stem of a tree.

veneer A thin layer of beautiful or expensive wood that is stuck on to cheaper wood.

wood The substance of which trees are made.

Index